Published by:

Pietas Publications
Waynesboro, Virginia, USA
web: www.jasperburns.com
email: pietas@jasperburns.com

THE NECESSARY NERD

Essential Stereotypes in the Basic Human Group

By Jasper Burns

THE NECESSARY NERD
Essential Stereotypes in the Basic Human Group

Contents

Introduction - 9

Chapter 1: Stereotypes in the Basic Human Group - 11

    What is the Basic Human Group? - 11

    Animal Parallels - 12

Chapter 2: Stereotypes in Contemporary Society - 15

Chapter 3: Human Stereotypes - 17

    Creative Stereotypes - 19

        Artist (Visionary) Stereotype - 19

        Craftsman Stereotype - 19

        Nerd/Geek Stereotype - 20

        Shaman/Seer/Healer Stereotype - 22

        Storyteller Stereotype - 22

    Didactic Stereotypes - 23

        Critical Stereotype - 23

        Preacher Stereotype - 23

        Teacher Stereotype - 24

    Leadership Stereotypes - 25

        Boss Stereotype - 25

        Boss's Assistant Stereotype - 26

        Enforcer/Thug Stereotype - 27

        Fanboy/Cheerleader Stereotype - 28

        Hero Stereotype - 28

Leader Stereotype - 29

Rebel Stereotype - 30

Reclusive Stereotypes - 31

Animal Whisperer Stereotype - 31

Hermit Stereotype - 31

Resource Stereotypes - 32

Banker/Accountant/Merchant Stereotype - 32

Control Freak/Neat Freak Stereotype - 32

Risk Taker Stereotype - 33

Salesman Stereotype - 33

Security Stereotypes - 34

Bellicose Stereotype - 34

Busy Body Stereotype - 35

Cop/Soldier Stereotype - 35

Criminal Stereotype - 36

Mediator Stereotype - 36

Strategist Stereotype - 37

Whistle-blower Stereotype - 37

Sex and Reproduction Stereotypes - 38

Beauty Queen Stereotype - 38

Breeder Stereotype - 39

Flirt Stereotype - 40

Gay/Transgender/Bisexual Stereotype - 40

Sexual Adventurer Stereotype - 41

Social Stereotypes - 42

Activist Stereotype - 42

Addict Stereotype - 42

Bi-Polar Stereotype - 43

Comedian Stereotype - 44

Disabled Stereotype - 44

Group Mother Stereotype - 45

Jackass/Pest/Prankster Stereotype - 46

Nurse/Doctor/Nutritionist Stereotype - 46

Worker Stereotypes - 47

Drudge/Tireless Laborer Stereotype - 47

Solitary Worker Stereotype - 47

Regular Folk Stereotype - 48

Emily May Praeger
"Preggers"

"Woo'd at haste, wed at leisure"
Out sick a lot . . . "I must of missed that period!" . . . early morning lav passes . . . cries in Home Ec . . . Emily May is busting out all over . . . excused from gym . . . nothin' says lovin' like somethin' in the oven . . . "Dibs on your pickles?"

Future Homemakers 4; Knitting Club 4.

Gilbert Bunsen Scrabbler
"Univac"

"The square of the hypotenuse equals the sum of the squares of the adjacent sides"
Big on trig . . . black lace-ups . . . always prepared . . . lime-green short-sleeve shirts with little notches at the arm . . . slide rule tie clip . . . "Mr. Machine" . . . different color socks . . . takes notes at lunch . . . don't you wish everybody did? . . . "Me sir, I know!" . . . studies in study hall.

Salutatorian; Honor Roll 1,2,3,4; Slipsticks 1,2,3,4; Winner *Time* Magazine Current Events Contest; State Science Fair Honorable Mention; Chess Club 2,3; Stamp Club 1,2; "Math'd Marvels" 1,2,3,4; Radio Club 3,4; Paraboleers 1,2,4; Insect Club 2; Reptile Club 2; Spider Club 1,3; Rocketry Club 1,2,3,4; Grade Average 99.9997; Full 4-Yr. Scholarship, United States War College.

Purdy Lee Spackle
"Psycho"

"He's a rebel . . ."
Uncontrollable bursts of enthusiasm . . . lots of attention getting qualities . . . actions speak louder than words . . . Angelina Staccato's initials carved in his arm . . . a doer, not a talker . . . often leaves school to take trips downtown . . . waiting for Fungus in the parking lot . . . a man of action . . . Arkansas toad sticker . . . waiting for Zippy in the parking lot . . . arresting personality . . . waiting for Swish in the parking lot . . . moody but well-respected.

Newcomer from Juvenile Work Farm High; Kar Klub 4.

Faun Laurel Rosenberg
"Weirdo"

"She marches to a different drummer"
Free spirit . . . artsy-craftsy-spooky-kooky . . . collects Burl Ives records . . . reads books . . . "You should call them Negroes!" . . . thinks Joan Baez can sing! . . . irons her hair . . . future Freedom Rider . . . black tights and jumpers . . . Peace Corps after college.

Hootenanny Club 4; Arbor Day Committee 3,4; *Leaf & Squib* 1,2,3,4; Drama Club 1,3,4; Pouchinellos 3; Mask & Wig 2,3; Guitar Club 4; Clay Pot Society 3,4; *Kaleidoscope* 2,3,4.

Maria Teresa Spermatozoa
"Quickie"

"I never met a man I didn't like"
It's what's up front that counts . . . low-priced spread . . . "Did you wash your hands?" . . . promise her anything but give her a Pez . . . S.W.A.F. . . . Jayvee Tongue-Wrestling Champ! . . . "Are you sure you washed your hands?" . . . P.D.A. . . . good ball handler . . . built like a brick dog house . . . can really do "the jerk!"

Girls' Bowling 2.

21

Sample page from the "National Lampoon 1964 High School Yearbook Parody", by P. J. O'Rourke, Doug Kenney, and David Kaestle, Copyright 1974, 1979.

Introduction

Way back in 1974, when I wasn't all that far removed from high school (class of '70), I picked up a copy of the brilliant publication "National Lampoon 1964 High School Yearbook Parody", by P. J. O'Rourke, Doug Kenney, and David Kaestle. This hilarious spoof inspired the movie "National Lampoon's Animal House" and serves as a tongue-in-cheek time capsule for baby boomers, filled with cultural references and satire that still bring back memories, cringe-worthy and otherwise.

The parody, in typical 1960s' yearbook format, begins with photographs of actors representing stereotypical teachers and students. The familiar teenage icons are all there – the nerd, the quarterback, the cheerleader, the dreamy artist, the bully, the criminal, and so on. I laughed at the exaggerated biographical details and portrait poses, but what struck me most indelibly was that I knew these people! I recognized personality types that were very familiar from my own high school experiences

During the past forty years, I have witnessed a succession of younger generations come along. Though each has its distinctive style and forms of expression, I see the same general types that I knew in my youth. Indeed, most of the stereotypes in the National Lampoon yearbook are still instantly recognizable, demonstrating their continuing relevance. It occurred to me that, transcending cultural change, there are basic human stereotypes that exist in every human society – and which must have adaptive value for the species or they would not be so persistent and widespread.

Of course, individual human beings are extremely complex and can't be defined by these stereotypes. A person may resemble different stereotypes at different stages of their lives and possess the qualities of several stereotypes at any given time. Also, the influences of culture and conditioning, both intentional and unintentional, may deter a person from expressing traits that come naturally to them. Conversely, individuals may emulate stereotypes that do not suit them because of the associated social or economic advantages.

I believe that many personality traits that are commonly labelled mental diseases, personality disorders, mistakes of Nature, or simply "uncool" are in fact highly adaptive and necessary for a complete and healthy human group. Nature does have its failed experiments and human beings can be damaged by numerous congenital and environmental factors, so not all traits are advantageous. However, if a stereotype (combination of traits) is widespread and persists over time, then it probably has adaptive value (or is genetically linked to a trait or traits with adaptive value) and should be respected and supported as necessary for the health and survival of the human community.

Chapter 1: Stereotypes in the Basic Human Group

Most commonly recognized human stereotypes have obvious value to human society. Leaders are essential to activities requiring planning and cooperation. Worry warts are more likely to remain alert for the approach of enemies. Reckless individuals may endanger themselves but do great service to the group by meeting external threats or exploring new resources. Each stereotype has traits and tendencies that contribute to the survival of the whole.

However – to the high school mentality at least - there is a tendency to think that there are only alpha males and females - and failed alpha males and females; the latter being somehow deficient and forced to make the best of less glamorous roles and identities. In other words, everyone is an alpha in a perfect society and all other stereotypes represent failed alphas. After all, everyone wants to be popular, powerful, and good-looking, right?

However, a society comprised entirely of quarterbacks and beauty queens wouldn't function well – nor would a society of wannabe quarterbacks and beauty queens. History and common sense show that a wide variety of basic personality types are necessary for the efficient functioning and development of human society. Even small societies need to have at least one representative of each stereotype in order to have the best chance of survival. There is no high or low in this diversity of types – each stereotype has a vital role to perform.

What is the Basic Human Group?

If human stereotypes have adaptive significance, then they should all be based on genetically inheritable traits and they should all be present within the basic human group. But what is the "basic human group"? How many individuals are necessary for a "band of humans" to have all the necessary stereotypes needed for survival?

In the 1990s, British anthropologist Robin Dunbar suggested a "cognitive limit to the number of people with whom one can maintain stable social relationships. These are relationships in which an individual knows who each person is and how each person relates to every other person." This number is based on physiological considerations and is an extrapolation of observed group sizes in other primates. The so-called "Dunbar's Number" – which may be interpreted as the maximum size of the basic human group – is proposed to lie between 100 and 250, with an estimated mean of 150.

Dunbar supported this number with studies of village sizes throughout history. For example, he found that 150 was the average population of Neolithic settlements and that Hutterite communities tended to split when they exceeded that number.

Interestingly, the Wikipedia list of "lost tribes" - isolated groups of people who live outside of the larger society - provides population estimates for 46 societies. The average number of members for each tribe is 157 – consistent with Dunbar's estimate.

If we can define the basic stereotypes of human nature and assume that 150 is the approximate size of a "complete" human society, then we can postulate how many individuals of each basic type is likely to be present in that society. In Chapter 3, I have taken a stab at defining the stereotypes and estimating the number for each.

Animal Parallels

There are many examples of physical and behavioral variation in animal societies. Anyone who has had more than one dog, more than one cat, or even more than one goldfish knows that each individual is psychologically unique. It may also be that animal personality stereotypes exist. Individual pets often behave in ways that "remind" their owners of other animals they have known.

Perhaps the most familiar example of polymorphism in a complex animal society is the one found among ants. Everyone knows

12

that there are workers and soldiers and queens. There may be dramatic size and behavioral differences among workers which correlate to different roles in the community. The bodies of the largest workers in some species may have a dry weight 500 times greater than those of the smallest workers. Some individuals in the colony may have enlarged heads and mandibles, which make them effective defenders or aggressors ("soldier ants") while others may become living storage vessels, allowing their abdomens to become distended with a quantity of liquid food ("repletes" among the "honeypot ants"). And then, of course, there are the queens: much larger than the other ants and the only reproducing female (or females, as there may be more than one) in an ant colony. There may or may not be male ants in an ant society.

Social hierarchies and role differentiation are also features of primate communities and, though less well-studied, also exist among prairie dogs, turkey flocks, wolf packs, and other animal societies in which cooperation is necessary for survival.

A theory of human personality traits, known as the "Five Factor Model", recognizes five basic parameters: openness, conscientiousness, extraversion, agreeableness, and neuroticism. There have been successful attempts to recognize individual variations for these factors in chimpanzees, gorillas, and orangutans. Variations in personality have also been seen in macaques, langurs, and vervet monkeys. These and other studies have demonstrated the obvious: there is variability in animal personalities that is not determined only by age and gender.

Chapter 2: Stereotypes in Contemporary Society

If the ideal assortment of human stereotypes is adapted for a basic human group of around 150 individuals, what happens when societies greatly exceed that number? Competition and cooperation are possible, both of which may be of benefit to the group. However, in complex modern societies, individuals must compete with public figures who dominate their stereotypes through government institutions and popular culture, forcing their local counterparts to resort to fantasy, fandom, or other roles. The high school hero is usurped by professional athletes, military heroes, and movie characters; the natural boss by corporate CEOs and heads of state; and the beauty queen by famous models, singers, and actresses.

Complex society also distorts human behavior because roles are inherited because of wealth or family connections, so inappropriate individuals inherit specific favored roles rather than earning them through personal qualifications. However, this is offset by the opportunities in large-scale societies for extreme specialization.

Stereotypes are often most pronounced and recognizable in high schools because these represent artificial "communities" of limited population in which individuals are able to assume their natural archetypal roles. The high school quarterback and head cheerleader are at the pinnacle of a closed society, though they will likely lose their preeminence when they graduate.

Unfortunately, there is a high school-like obsession with the "ideal person" in modern society. Therapies and medications of many kinds are used to rid individuals of the fearfulness, restlessness, social awkwardness, tendency to take risks, hypersensitivity, and insensitivity that can make life in modern society difficult. While some of these qualities may be signs of stress, trauma, or physical ailments, in their healthiest forms they may be of potential value to the individual and to society. Therefore, it is important to recognize and value all stereotypes and human diversity in general.

Typically, every individual in a small, primitive, "tribal" human society must be a generalist in order to survive. Though some individuals will take the lead in certain areas, each person will need to learn the basics of acquiring food and shelter. Beyond these essential activities, there is usually plenty of time for specialization – for assuming one's natural role.

However, the individual in a complex society must specialize and rely on others for basic needs and services. The fact that there are fewer opportunities in modern societies for some stereotypes - such as heroes, shamans, and artists – means that there are many frustrated "wannabes". Many of these individuals seek consolation in fantasy games, sports, daydreams, movies, novels, addictions, misanthropy, and antisocial behavior.

Chapter 3: Human Stereotypes

The stereotypes described on the following pages represent specific combinations of tendencies, talents, and areas of activity that are important for human group health and survival. Ideally, all stereotypes will be represented by one or more members of any complete human group.

Two kinds of stereotype are included which overlap with each other: the social role stereotypes and the personality type stereotypes. The former are basic roles in society and the latter describe important traits that may be found in a variety of social stereotypes. For example, one individual may be a craftsman or banker or criminal while also being a comedian or worry wart. The social role and personality stereotypes are listed together because in larger, more advanced societies, a personality type can actually become a social role. For example, one can become a professional comedian or busy body (e. g. gossip columnist) in modern civilized society – something that would be impossible in a small primitive community.

An estimated number of people for each stereotype in a "basic human group" of 150 individuals is given. These numbers are highly speculative. They are based on the assumption that three generations are living concurrently at any given time and do not take differential mortality for different stereotypes into consideration. The total number of individuals for all listed stereotypes far exceeds 150 as individuals will often possess the qualities of more than one stereotype, as discussed in the preceding paragraph.

It should also be borne in mind that people may migrate from one stereotype to another as they age (e.g. Beauty Queen to Group Mother, Hero to Boss). Also, it is assumed that individuals are able to express their natural traits without the interference of inheritance, conditioning, social stigmatism, or other artificial processes. Indeed, the expression of some stereotypes may be suppressed by the dominance of outside groups, periods of extreme hardship, or the influence of oppressive religious, social (e.g. caste, class, or family restrictions), or other cultural factors. Also, certain stereotypes may be encouraged by periods of rampant innovation or thwarted by periods of extreme social and cultural conservatism.

Some societies may appear to lack one or more of these stereotypes. This may be the result of active discouragement of certain traits (e.g. some sexual orientations), resulting in the suppression of those tendencies by the individuals who have them. In extreme cases, societies may punish or attempt to remove individuals with certain traits without realizing that those traits are beneficial to the group.

For example, we may wonder if one of the reasons ancient Sparta in Greece lagged behind Athens in cultural and technological achievement was because the Spartans systematically exposed their physically imperfect offspring, selecting for physical traits but possibly against intellectual and psychological ones. Were the Spartans killing off their nerds and artists and creating a society of sports heroes and cheerleaders, thereby stymieing cultural and technological development?

Some stereotypes may be considered aberrant in some or most societies (e.g. bi-polar, worry wart, gay, hermit stereotypes). However, if these types persist over time and across cultures, they almost certainly are adaptive or are genetically linked to adaptive traits and should therefore be respected and supported. The fact that they are considered pathological – and may be detrimental to the well-being of some individuals – is often due to ostracism or failure of a society to understand the nature and importance of the stereotype and to provide opportunities for healthy expression.

The following list is a rough draft. Further consideration may argue for combining types or adding new ones, but it is a starting point for conversation. It should be said that individuals named as examples for each stereotype are listed only for illustrative purposes. No human being can be defined by a stereotype; all persons have features from more than one and all have numerous non-stereotypical characteristics that are all their own.

Creative Stereotypes

Artist (Visionary) Stereotype

These are the inspired artists, musicians, dancers, poets, actors, or writers (in literate societies) who create iconic stories, images, songs, or performances that cement and inspire the society, though not always in their lifetimes. The inspired artist tends to be aloof, misunderstood, and/or poorly integrated in the group. They are often prone to anxiety because of a lack of conscious control over their inspiration and productivity. Also, they may be insecure because of the perceived impracticality and subjective value of their contributions to the group and are often very sensitive to criticism. Their anxiety may lead to excessive indulgence in intoxicants or otherwise self-damaging behavior.

Importance to Group: These artists may be a burden to the group at times but may also create symbols that inspire or define its highest ideals. Their "otherness" may inspire other group members to be more innovative and individualistic.

Proposed Number in Basic Group: 6 (two per generation)

Examples: John Lennon, Leonardo da Vinci, Michael Jackson, Jimi Hendrix, Frida Kahlo, Sarah Bernhardt, Rainer Maria Rilke

Craftsman Stereotype

These are the specialized masters of skills and crafts, including methods of construction, storage, transportation, farming, warfare, etc. The emphasis is on knowledge and skill rather than originality, though they may introduce important innovations and their work may attain the status of high art. They are more skilled than the typical worker, but are more balanced and practical than the nerds and are not geeky. This stereotype includes master potters, blacksmiths, builders, weavers, mechanics, tool-makers, and non-visionary artists. Unlike the visionary artist, who is largely dependent on subconscious, highly personal inspiration, these master craftsmen are hard-headed and primarily involved in applying principles rather than looking for novel, individualistic expression.

Importance to Group: These members are vital for applying and preserving the technological skills and crafts that are essential to group defense and the creation of shelter, clothing, tools, and food production.

Proposed Number in Basic Group: 15 (five per generation including apprentices)

Examples: Usually not famous except locally. Norman Rockwell, Hephaestus, Antonio Stradivari, Michelangelo, Peter Carl Fabergé

Nerd/Geek Stereotype

A nerd is defined here as an individual with an obsessive interest in an academic or technological subject and with some degree of social awkwardness and introversion that encourages their pre-occupation with that subject. Nerds are highly creative and original thinkers and devise new ideas and discover new methods or explanations for physical phenomena. They often work together with master craftsmen to test theories and create new specialized tools or weapons based on theoretical models. They may be so enamored of knowledge that they fail to see the negative effects of technological innovation.

They tend to be physically uncoordinated and are often near-sighted. This last association may seem to be over-generalizing, but a tendency to myopia might be appropriate for close work with gadgets, tools, reading, etc., especially in societies without the technology for vision correction (almost all of human history). The following from an article in the December 20, 1988 New York Times reporting on research at the Danish Institute of Myopia Research may be relevant here:

In general, people who are nearsighted do better on intelligence tests and achieve higher educational levels than those who are not, but the traditional explanation -that reading promotes nearsightedness in genetically susceptible people - may not be correct, Danish scientists say. Instead, they suggest, "visual exploration of the near environment" from birth may be associated with both higher intelligence and nearsightedness later in life.

Importance to Group: Often discover new materials, tools, technologies, or insights that increase the well-being and security of the group.

Proposed Number in Basic Group: 9 (three per generation)

Examples: Steven Hawking, Albert Einstein, Bill Gates, Steve Jobs

THE NERD

Shaman/Seer/Healer/Mystic Stereotype

Similar to visionary artists in that they are guided by subconscious inspiration, but their creativity deals more with psychological states and practices. They have a need to "know" the unknown and are often drawn to mind-altering substances and activities. They are often interested in arcane knowledge and group mythology and may claim to be in touch with spirits of animals and ancestors or divine beings. In primitive societies, these individuals may also be healers or teachers because of their vivid imaginations and access to the subconscious, but in more complex societies these roles (doctors, psychologists, preachers, etc.) tend to require specialized training and are closed to the intuitive practitioner, except in alternative contexts. Their outward behavior is often unconventional, but varies widely depending on culture.

Importance to Group: May help define group metaphysical beliefs and explain natural phenomena. Diagnose and treat psychologically-based ailments and ease emotional discomfort. Often have unique insights into the spiritual health of the group.

Proposed Number in Basic Group: – 6 (one each sex per generation)

Examples: Black Elk, John the Baptist, St. Francis of Assisi, Carl Jung, Aleister Crowley, Jesus Christ, Gautama Buddha

Storyteller Stereotype

These promote the cohesion and cultural identity of the group by retelling its history and legends. These are creative artists who do more than just compile facts and genealogies – they turn history into instructive and inspiring allegories for personal and group success and fulfillment. They may also invent fictional stories that reflect cultural experiences and values and inspire the group in a similar way. These differ from visionary artists in their preoccupation with history and society, or their fictional counterparts, rather than on themselves. They tend to focus on the past rather than the present and future.

Importance to Group: Define and refine group moral values and traditions by illustrating these principles through story and legend. This guides group behavior and inspires individuals by reminding them of ideals and past glories.

Proposed Number in Basic Group: 2 (one plus apprentice)

Examples: Homer, Vyasa, Hans Christian Andersen, Joseph Jacobs, Jakob and Wilhelm Grimm, J. R. R. Tolkien, William Shakespeare

Didactic Stereotypes

Critical Stereotype

These individuals are instinctively judgmental. They reflexively respond to almost any narrative or behavior with "What you should have done is…." Closely related to teachers, they are usually loners. If their critiques are humorous, they may perform roles similar to comedians, but are more likely to be serious and negative.

Importance to Group: They often provide feedback that allows group members to improve or gain new perspectives on their work or behavior. If too aggressive or misguided, they may perform the same functions as the "Jackass" social stereotype.

Proposed Number in Basic Group: 3 (one per generation)

Examples: Bill Maher, Gore Vidal, William F. Buckley. Jr., Joan Rivers

Preacher Stereotype

They are thoroughly committed to a belief system or cause and always looking for audiences to hear their version of the truth or to chastise those who don't subscribe to it. In cultures with sophisticated ethical or moral codes and religious dogmatism, preachers

THE CRITIC

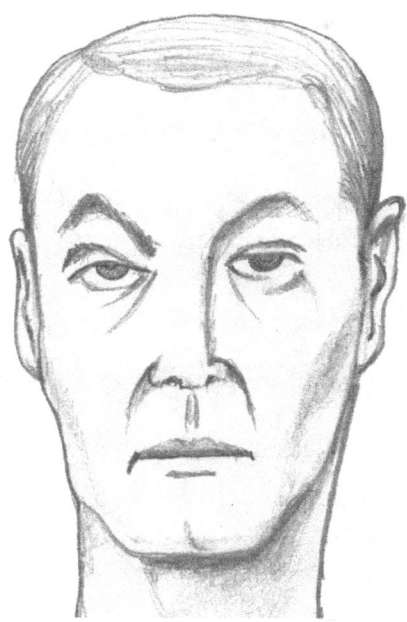

may become leaders, especially if a society has strayed from its ideals. Similar to teachers in style, but their goal is moral improvement. Those preachers who seek to uplift themselves may become philosophers.

Importance to Group: They continually remind group members of established beliefs and codes of behavior, serving as the embodiment of group conscience.

Proposed Number in Basic Group: 3 (one per generation)

Examples: Martin Luther King, Jr., Savaronola, Mahatma Gandhi, John Brown, Confucius, Socrates, Pythagoras, Thomas Aquinas

<u>Teacher Stereotype</u>

In addition to passing on basic knowledge, they are defenders of the status quo and conventional wisdom. They may become preachers if the religion is defined by a book or involves a rigid moral code. They may be pedantic nitpickers and language cops and defend tradition against random innovation or error. They generally dislike nonconformists and are suspicious of innovation or radical new ideas, but there are important exceptions.

Importance to Group: Important for cultural cohesion, persistence of basic knowledge and skills, and cultural continuity. The best of them may be inspirational.

Proposed Number in Basic Group: 9 (three per generation)

Examples: Plato, Aristotle, Maria Montessori, Noah Webster, Friedrich Froebel

Leadership Stereotypes

Boss Stereotype

J. R. R. Tolkien said: "The most improper job of any man... is bossing other men. Not one in a million is fit for it, and least of all those who seek the opportunity." Nevertheless, bosses are inevitable and necessary in human societies. Natural bosses are clever, calculating, manipulative, and good at controlling people (including heroes) by exploiting their strengths and weaknesses, for good or ill. They are good judges of character. Bosses are most effective during times of peace and stability and may be expendable in times of danger or upheaval when leaders or heroes become more important. Bosses are frequently the most powerful and prosperous members of a society but are generally not the leaders. They are often the "powers behind the throne" and usually indifferent to public recognition and praise. They often lack social skills and prefer to manipulate natural leaders. Bosses are patient, steady of purpose, and have nerves of steel. They see the "big picture" and are often ruthless.

Importance to Group: They manipulate the group's talents and focus group energies on getting things done.

Proposed Number in Basic Group: 3 (one per generation)

Examples: Agamemnon, Joseph Stalin, Don Corleone, Richard Nixon, Dick Cheney

THE BOSS

Boss's Assistant Stereotype

These are the boss's "right hand men", hard-headed operatives such as lawyers, managers, and negotiators. They are more pragmatic and cerebral than enforcers and fanboys but also support the status quo and adhere to powerful individuals.

Importance to Group: Enable the bosses to organize and maintain the power structure and group productivity.
Proposed Number in Basic Group: 6 (two per generation)

Examples: Roy Cohn, H. R. Haldeman, Heinrich Himmler

Enforcer/Thug Stereotype

Often physically intimidating but not too bright, they support and protect heroes, bosses, and leaders. They abhor nonconformity, support the status quo and are often bullies. Left to their own devices, they may become criminals but are usually controlled by loyalty to legitimate leaders. May become cops or soldiers.

Importance to Group: Help leaders lead by intimidating other members of the group into cooperation.

Proposed Number in Basic Group: 9 (three per generation)

Examples: Little John, Hamish Campbell in Braveheart, Chewbacca, Luca Brasi

THE THUG

Fanboy/Cheerleader Stereotype

These individuals are under the spell of a hero, leader, or ideology and have a cult-like loyalty and enthusiasm for them. They often have a gift for persuasive praise, using words to support leaders or dogma and manipulate potential followers with words much as enforcers use physical intimidation. May be propagandists, advocates, and proselytizers and may be mercenary in their choice of heroes and causes. Related to the salesman stereotype, but their wares are people and ideas rather than products.

Importance to Group: They bring group attention to outstanding individuals or causes and help refine and express group ideals. They may also motivate and inspire group members who want to earn their praise and attention.

Proposed Number in Basic Group: 6 (two per generation)

Examples: Bob Costas, Joseph Goebbels, Bill Simmons

Hero Stereotype

A charismatic, physically gifted athlete and/or warrior. He is the natural leader in the physical and social activities of youth. However, he may not have leadership qualities beyond his physical gifts. Often reckless and may die young; he is desired by females as beauty queens are desired by young males. Often supported by adoring fanboys and loyal enforcers/thugs.

Importance to Group: He inspires others to action by example. His recklessness may benefit the group and his sexual attractiveness may awaken sexual feeling in young women and gay men.

Proposed Number in Basic Group: 3 (one per generation)

Examples: Achilles, Mickey Mantle, John F. Kennedy, Alexander the Great, David Beckham, Joe Montana, Michael Jordan

Leader Stereotype

This is a critically important stereotype but often problematic in complex societies. True leaders are not common as too many leaders could split the group. In modern societies, leadership positions may only be available to individuals with social advantages and a power base, or with personal charisma and media savvy, which may be detrimental to society.

Natural leaders are good communicators, listeners, and persuaders, often have superior social and intellectual qualities, but also have the common touch. There is evidence that leadership qualities may be linked with superior height. People may be more willing to follow an ideal or imposing physical type. However, other attributes (e.g. speechmaking ability or fearlessness) may suffice. Leaders crave the support and admiration of followers and become more confident and even more capable when more people are behind them.

THE HERO

In complex societies, leaders arise in different segments of society – political, economic, religious, etc. There is often a narcissistic component to the leader psychology. Self-absorbed individuals may inspire other members of the group to engage in grandiose or daring projects intended to glorify themselves but which are also of benefit to the group. A society may be swept into greatness by the pretensions of one narcissistic individual. A leader may be indifferent to the opinions and feelings of others, which may be necessary to push through a challenging or unpopular agenda.

Importance to Group: Makes important decisions and directs some kinds of cooperative group activity. A focal point for group aspirations.

Proposed Number in Basic Group: 6 (two per generation)

Examples: Julius Caesar, Franklin Roosevelt, Bill Clinton, Adolf Hitler, Nero (narcissistic), Alexander the Great, Napoleon, Louis XIV, Douglas MacArthur

Rebel Stereotype

The rebel is instinctively at odds with the established order and conventional behavior. Generally, he or she has an alternative belief system and/or lifestyle. The rebel may be motivated by pride, resentment, or ambition as easily as by a desire for social progress and often would like to be a boss and may ultimately become one.

Importance to Group: Heightens and focuses discontentment with the status quo, which may bring about necessary change.

Proposed Number in Basic Group: 6 (one plus apprentice per generation)

Examples: James Dean, Fidel Castro, Vladimir Lenin, John Brown, Malcolm X, Woody Guthrie

Reclusive Stereotypes

Animal Whisperer Stereotype

These individuals are drawn to be keepers and/or breeders of animals, hunting specialists, or veterinarians and serve as bridges between species. The relationships between animals and human beings, as predator and prey, producer and consumer, and cooperative partners have always been vital to human survival. Certain individuals have a heightened awareness of animal nature and the ability to communicate with them or interpret their behavior. Some humans are actually more at ease in the company of animals than other humans.

Importance to Group: It may be that such individuals were indispensable in the processes of animal domestication, breeding, and development of training methods and that without them horses, dogs, and carrier pigeons may never have served man. A less common variation of this stereotype is focused on plants and plant cultivation.

Proposed Number in Basic Group: 3 (one per generation)

Examples: Jane Goodall, Dian Fossey, Konrad Lorenz, Gregor Mendel

Hermit Stereotype

May be an antisocial rebel or just socially inept and unable to deal with people. Lives outside the group and participates in few or none of its activities. Some hermits have shamanic tendencies and live apart to pursue spiritual practices.

Importance to Group: As hermits tend to be conservative, they may preserve old ways of doing things. They may also help restore the population if the young males are reduced or wiped out by warfare, accident, or disease. Those who attain wisdom may guide and inspire the group through limited contact or from a distance.

Proposed Number in Basic Group: 3 (one per generation)

Examples: Jeremiah Johnson, St. Jerome, Ramana Maharshi, Julian of Norwich, Baal Shem Tov

Resource Stereotypes

Banker/Accountant/Merchant Stereotype

These group members are detail-oriented and good at appraising the value and availability of goods. They may be merchants, brokers, or collectors and controllers of important artifacts or records.

Importance to Group: They keep track of, organize, and manipulate group resources and distribute them as needed. They may also call into account those who exceed their needs or are dishonest and can warn the group about potential shortfalls.

Proposed Number in Basic Group: 6 (two per generation)

Examples: Warren Buffett, J. P. Morgan, Alan Greenspan, Sam Walton, Jim Cramer

Control Freak/Neat Freak Stereotype

These individuals take great interest in the efficient and orderly maintenance of group resources and infrastructure. They abhor disorganization and decay. May become obsessive-compulsive.

Importance to Group: Important for hygiene and to ensure that all equipment necessary for defense and survival is functioning, readily available, and in good order.

Proposed Number in Basic Group: 3 (one per generation)

Examples: Martha Stewart, Niles and Frasier Crane

Risk Taker Stereotype

These are often reckless loners and not team players like the hero, though often just as physically gifted. They excel at hunting, fighting, or some other physical skill. Often pursue solo sports or activities and may be racecar drivers, tennis players, gamblers, mountain climbers, explorers, body builders, snipers, spies.

Importance to Group: Their outstanding abilities and dare-devil exploits may inspire others or benefit the group by opening up new resources or possibilities or by eliminating threats.

Proposed Number in Basic Group: 6 (one per sex per generation – but they are often short-lived)

Examples: Ted Williams, John McEnroe, Evel Knievel, Wilt Chamberlain, Roald Amundsen, Dean Potter, James Bond, Daniel Boone, Hercules

Salesman Stereotype

They are always on the make for a profit or major deal. Related to the banker/merchant stereotype, they are less specialized and motivated more by the thrill and challenge of making a sale than by resource management and distribution. A difficulty in modern society is that a disproportionate number of people are employed in retail who are not salesmen by nature and who have no stake in the enterprise. They are expected to "smile and sell" but their hearts aren't in it.

Importance to Group: They facilitate the movement of goods and services through the group and often come up with creative ways of using or distributing resources. They may often popularize new products or services through enthusiastic salesmanship.

Proposed Number in Basic Group: 6 (1 per sex per generation)

Examples: Dale Carnegie, Ron Popeil, Joe Girard, Billy Graham, Kim Kardashian

THE SALESWOMAN

Security Stereotypes

Bellicose Stereotype

Fight or flight. Sometimes it is better to fight. Many times in history, overwhelming odds have been overcome. However, the armless and legless knight in "Monty Python and the Holy Grail" may have taken this stereotype a little too far. These group members are highly competitive and often push other members to reach their potentials. Often similar to rebels in their behavior but are thoroughly identified with the establishment.

Importance to Group: They embolden and persuade others to face threats and inflame warlike passions. They may also stir up confrontations within the group, which may be necessary and cathartic.

Proposed Number in Basic Group: 3 (one per generation)

Examples: Michael Jordan, Winston Churchill, Donald Rumsfeld, Cato the Elder

Busy Body/Informer/Journalist/Chatterbox Stereotype

Nosy neighbors may notice that your house is on fire before you do. In modern societies, these highly communicative individuals keep up an endless real-time chatter on social media, television, blogs, and Facebook. Almost nothing escapes their notice and very few matters are not disclosed.

Importance to Group: These individuals pry, spy, and notice things others don't and then keep everyone informed, whether they like it or not. They become even more important in larger, more complex societies when much activity is hidden from view.

Proposed Number in Basic Group: 6 (two per generation)

Examples: Joan Rivers, Regis Philbin and Kathy Lee Gifford, Ellen DeGeneres, Bill O'Reilly, Mike Wallace, Christiane Amanpour

Cop/Soldier Stereotype

They are related to the enforcers, but their loyalty is to principles and the common good rather than to specific leaders, bosses, or causes.

Importance to Group: These individuals protect the group from internal and external threats and enforce laws or social codes.

Proposed Number in Basic Group: 6 (two per generation)

Examples: Elliot Ness, Frank Serpico, Matt Dillon, John McCain, Kojak, Lieutenant Columbo, Sergeant Joe Friday

Criminal Stereotype

These individuals are cheats, liars, and thieves. Some are actually rebels who feel justified in their actions because of injustices done to them or others or are attracted to mayhem and chaos for ideological reasons. Others simply get a thrill out of criminal behavior or are motivated by a desire for power or easy money. Like bosses and leaders, they may be served by enforcers and thugs. This stereotype could be divided into several as it represents a broad range of types with different psychologies ranging from petty thieves to psychopathic serial killers.

Importance to Group: They mix things up, redistribute wealth, and keep the group on alert. They may also inspire improvements in security and be useful in espionage against rival groups.

Proposed Number in Basic Group: 6 (one per sex per generation)

Examples: Al Capone, John Dillinger, Charles Manson, Ted Kaczynski, Ted Bundy

Mediator Stereotype

These individuals promote peace and harmony, both among individuals and competing groups. They abhor confrontation and violence and explore all possible avenues for compromise and the resolution of conflict.

Importance to Group: Help avoid or minimize damaging conflict between community members and groups.

Proposed Number in Basic Group: 6 (two per generation)

Examples: Jimmy Carter, Mahatma Gandhi, Pope John Paul II, Mikhail Gorbachev, Nelson Mandela

Strategist Stereotype

These individuals have unusual deductive and analytical abilities. They are adept at recognizing threats and opportunities and planning successful ways of dealing with them. They can often see the connections between apparently unrelated factors. They may be detectives, generals, long range planners, logicians, and mathematicians. They are related to the boss's assistant stereotype, but are usually more independent and creative.

Importance to Group: Important in recognizing and avoiding or overcoming threats to group safety.

Proposed Number in Basic Group: 3 (one per generation)

Examples: Marcus Agrippa, Ulysses S. Grant, Robert E. Lee, Sherlock Holmes, George S. Patton, Hannibal, Julius Caesar

Whistle-blower/Worry Wart/Sentry Stereotype

These group members have an extreme awareness of possible threats and speak often and loudly about their fears. They are attuned to the physical surroundings, are suspicious of strangers, and may have unusually acute senses of sight, smell, and hearing.

Importance to Group: They are vital for group safety, with enhanced awareness of both internal and external threats, including shortage of necessary resources. However, they may often resemble the boy who cried "wolf" and are frequently ignored.

Proposed Number in Basic Group: 6 (one each sex per generation)

Examples: Barney Fife, John McCain, Paul Revere, Vedanta Shiva, Ralph Nader

WORRY WART

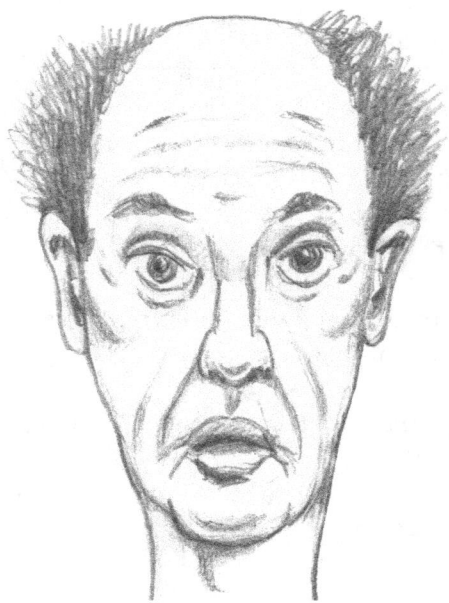

Sex and Reproduction Stereotypes

Beauty Queen Stereotype

The Homecoming queen, head cheerleader, movie star. She has beauty, grace, usually an outgoing personality, and is desired by many boys and men. In youth, like the male hero, she is the natural social leader among young women and may consort with the hero of her age group. Later, she often unites with a boss or leader in order to maintain her primacy among women or because the boss or leader has his pick of mates.

Importance to Group: She awakens sexual feelings among many males when young.

Proposed Number in Basic Group: 3 (one per generation)

Examples: Cameron Diaz, Helen of Troy, Marilyn Monroe, Ginger on Gilligan's Island, Angelina Jolie

BEAUTY QUEEN

Breeder Stereotype

These females have an abundance of children, usually starting at an early age, and most of their energies go into raising their brood. After their reproductive years end, they are often absorbed in helping to raise the next generation.

Importance to Group: Keep population up and often have enhanced intuition about physical and psychological factors. They may aid group cohesion and improve general mental and physical health.

Proposed Number in Basic Group: 18 (three each sex per generation)

Examples: Momma Walton, the Old Woman who lived in a shoe.

Flirt Stereotype

These group members are preoccupied with sexual relationships and are often matchmakers. They have a great interest in people and recognize connections and compatibilities that others don't. They are different from sexual adventurers, who are usually more determined and surreptitious in their activities.

Importance to Group: May arouse sexual feeling in the young and test bonds between partners.

Proposed Number in Basic Group: 6 (two per generation)

Examples: Mickey Rooney, George Sand, Groucho Marx, Julia Roberts, Mae West, David Letterman, Dolly Parton, Marilyn Monroe

Gay/Transgender/Bisexual Stereotype

They often have characteristics that are intermediate between genders or unique to their own orientation, such as distinctive creative abilities or insights. They are frequently spiritual leaders or shamans.

Importance to Group: Serve as bridges between the sexes. May allow sexual release with same anatomical sex members or emotional intimacy with members of the opposite sex without risk of pregnancy. May be negative examples for other members, thereby strengthening mainstream gender role behavior.

Proposed Number in Basic Group: 18 (three each sex per generation)

Examples: Elton John, Ellen DeGeneres, Liberace, K. D. Lang, RuPaul, Caitlyn Jenner

SEXUAL ADVENTURER

<u>Sexual Adventurer Stereotype</u>

As opposed to flirts, these seducers work quietly and are often driven in their pursuit of sexual liaisons and conquests.

Importance to Group: They mix up the gene pool and arouse the reproductive instincts of slow developers.

Proposed Number in Basic Group: 6 (one each sex per generation)

Examples: Casanova, Warren Beatty, Madonna, Errol Flynn, Cleopatra (as popularly imagined)

Social Stereotypes

Activist Stereotype

These group members tend to be highly sensitive and vocal about injustices. They do not withdraw like some sensitive types. Unlike rebels, they tend to seek retribution within the system and are often litigious.

Importance to Group: They may make the group aware of injustices and imbalances in resource distribution or treatment by more powerful members.

Proposed Number in Basic Group: 3 (one per generation)

Examples: Mahatma Gandhi, Martin Luther King, Jr., Gloria Steinem, Rosa Parks

Addict Stereotype

Though viewed as dysfunctional, this type is widespread and recorded for all cultures and periods of history and must therefore have value to the group. Before finding their drug of choice, these individuals are often highly agitated and ill-adapted.

The addict stereotype emphasizes internal sensations and is often exemplified by the most sensitive, introspective, and intuitive members of the group. In extreme cases, they may fill a role similar to that of the Disabled Stereotype (see below). Addicts may overcome their dependency and avoid the consequences of addiction, but even if they don't, they often make important contributions to the group, often as seers, artists, poets, or storytellers. It may be wondered if the creative contributions of the people listed below would have been as significant if they had always remained sober. This stereotype is distinct from those in which the addiction is to external experiences such as sex or gambling (see Risk-Taker and Sexual Adventurer stereotypes), though the traits are often found in the same individual.

Importance to Group: The drug of choice may induce quasi-religious experiences or special insights that are valued by the group. Emotional outbursts "under the influence" may bring controversies or injustices to the attention of the group at large.

Proposed Number in Basic Group: 6 (two per generation)

Examples: Judy Garland, Richard Burton, Samuel Coleridge, Elvis Presley, Keith Moon, Jim Morrison, Edgar Allen Poe, Janis Joplin, Whitney Houston

Bi-Polar Stereotype

Bi-polarity is viewed as a disorder and individuals with this condition are routinely medicated in modern society. However, this trait has occurred through human history and representative individuals have made vital contributions to society.

By definition, bi-polar individuals experience mood swings. They require the freedom to change their activities and surroundings suddenly and frequently – not always possible with the regimentation of school and full-time office jobs in modern societies. Bi-polar individuals often seek to create the variety they need through mind-altering substances or dramatic social behavior. Society might be much better served if they were given more slack and allowed to be inconsistent without being punished, medicated, or stigmatized for it. Bi-polarity is not actually a stereotype in and of itself. Rather, it is a trait that occurs in some individuals within almost every stereotype.

Importance to Group: The restlessness and creative energy of these people often produce vital contributions to the group in many areas, including the arts, spirituality, and various forms of leadership.

Proposed Number in Basic Group: 6 (two per generation)

Examples: Jim Carrey, Winston Churchill, Mel Gibson, Graham Greene, Ernest Hemingway, Vivien Leigh, Marilyn Monroe, Edvard Munch, Friedrich Nietzsche, Florence Nightingale, Phil Ochs, Sir Isaac Newton, William Pitt, Jackson Pollock, John Ruskin, Frank Sinatra, Mark Twain, Vincent van Gogh, Robin Williams, Brian Wilson, Virginia Woolf

Comedian Stereotype

These are gifted mimics and jokesters, generally the life of the party. They often have profound insights into the peculiarities of human nature and society. There are many flavors of this stereotype: some lighthearted and playful; others ideological and even revolutionary.

Importance to Group: They often lighten the mood and lessen tensions between group members. They also strengthen a sense of community within the group by revealing shared experiences, resentments, etc. and often bring social problems to light.

Proposed Number in Basic Group: 6 (two per generation)

Examples: Jim Carrey, Richard Pryor, Lucille Ball, Robin Williams, Lenny Bruce, George Carlin

Disabled Stereotype

Though this may not always be an intentional stereotype (determined by genetics), it is a persistent and valuable one. It includes a wide variety of congenital disabilities, though injury or disease may alter individuals so that they effectively assume this role.

Importance to Group: Increases generosity and protective instincts among group members. Some individuals make important contributions.

Proposed Number in Basic Group: 6 (1 per sex per generation)

Examples: Autistic, Down Syndrome, physically or mentally handicapped individuals. Helen Keller, Ray Charles, Stevie Wonder, Steven Hawking

Group Mother Stereotype

This mature female has great insight and empathy for most or all members of the group. She instinctively understands emotional and often physical needs and many members turn to her for advice and consolation, even as adults. Her nurturing and mediating skills help to keep everyone connected and in harmony. She may also serve as a matchmaker and social director. She may or may not have numerous children.

Importance to Group: Promotes peace and helps keep marginal members in the group by meeting their emotional needs and healing hurt feelings.

Proposed Number in Basic Group: 3 (one per generation)

Examples: Aunt Bee in Andy Griffith Show, Amma the Hugging Saint, Oprah Winfrey, Mary mother of Jesus, Eleanor Roosevelt

GROUP MOTHER

Jackass/Pest/Prankster Stereotype

These individuals keep group members off balance and more alert about group dynamics and challenges. They love to "get a rise" out of others and abhor stagnation or over-seriousness. Typically overbearing, over-loud, indiscreet, and often not as funny or clever as they think they are. May be comedians or the butts of comedians' jokes.

Importance to Group: They strengthen relationships by challenging them and may improve communication within the group. They often reveal secrets, which can be constructive.

Proposed Number in Basic Group: 3 (one per generation)

Examples: Howard Stern, Kanye West, Dennis Rodman, Jim Carrey

Nurse/Doctor/Nutritionist Stereotype

These individuals are fascinated by what promotes and threatens physical health. Many people have an intuitive feel for this, but may not be able to practice in modern society because they are out-competed by less-qualified individuals who seek the money and status involved, or who possess largely irrelevant intellectual gifts.

Importance to Group: Besides being adept at diagnosing and treating disease, they are knowledgeable about edible foods and beneficial herbs and other remedies.

Proposed Number in Basic Group: 6 (1 each sex per generation)

Examples: Hippocrates, Florence Nightingale, Mother Theresa, Albert Schweitzer, Clara Barton, William and Charles Mayo

Worker Stereotypes

Drudge/Tireless Laborer Stereotype

Like worker ants, these group members are workaholics by nature. They spend most of their time improving the group's surroundings or gathering resources.

Importance to Group: As these members work beyond the norm, they inspire or shame others to work harder.

Proposed Number in Basic Group: 12 (4 per generation)

Examples: Chris Mullin, Jimmy Carter, John Henry, Benjamin Franklin, Hillary Clinton

Solitary Worker Stereotype

There individuals are often reclusive or rebellious, but not hermits as they are still connected to and identified with the group. They prefer to work alone on projects of their own choosing and may be programmers, hunters, writers, artists, or inventors. Some are reckless amateurs who eschew formal training and may (or may not) break new ground by "re-inventing" better wheels.

Importance to Group: May discover important new resources, perspectives, or ways of doing things.

Proposed Number in Basic Group: 3 (one per generation)

Examples: Leonardo da Vinci, William Blake, J. K. Rowling, Albert Einstein, Mahatma Gandhi, Nikola Tesla

Regular Folk Stereotype

These numerous individuals are generalists rather than specialists, followers rather than leaders. They have no extreme qualities or skills but possess a balance of many. Regular folk may be geniuses of balance and stability. They have the ability to obey without rancor and can adjust readily to changes of leadership or direction.

Importance to Group: They do most of the labor in the group, both "blue color" and "white color", and they may take on other roles when needed as they have the potential for many things.

Proposed Number in Basic Group: 60 (10 each sex per generation)

Examples: John and Jane Doe

Books by Jasper Burns

The Necessary Nerd (Pietas Publications, 2015)

Trice Blessed (Pietas Publications, 2015)

Drawings by Jasper Burns (Pietas Publications, 2015)

Irish Hammered Pennies of Edward IV, Richard III, and Edward V (three editions) (Pietas Publications, 2009-15)

Inside (Pietas Publications, 1981, 2014)

P. B.'s Quick Index to Game Fish of the Chesapeake Bay (Pietas Publications, 2014)

Virginia Through Time (Pietas Publications, 2014)

Two Lucys in Europe (Pietas Publications, 2014)

A Lady in Jamaica (Pietas Publications, 2014)

Gale Hill: The Story of an Old Virginia Home (Pietas Publications, 2013)

Ammonite: An Eco-Fantasy (Pietas Publications, 2013)

Coin Stories (Pietas Publications, 2013)

Senior Moments (Pietas Publications, 2013)

Seeing God: Close Encounters of the Divine Kind (Pietas Publications, 2012)

Commodus and the Five Good Emperors (Pietas Publications, 2012)

Turtle Crossing (Pietas Publications, 2012)

Dreamweaving (Pietas Publications, 2012)

Roman Empresses (Pietas Publications, 2012)

Wisdom Illustrated (Pietas Publications, 2012)

Fossil Beach (Pietas Publications, 2012)

Bulla Felix: The Roman Robin Hood (Pietas Publications, 2011)

Great Women of Imperial Rome: Mothers and Wives of the Caesars (Routledge, 2007)

Fossil Dreams (Pietas Publications, 2007)

Selected Lives: The Autobiography of a Soul (Pietas Publications, 2006)

Vipsania: A Roman Odyssey (Pietas Publications, 2006)

Trilobites: Common Trilobites of North America (NatureGuide Books, 2000)

Exploring Fossils (Virginia Museum of Natural History, 1998)

Fossil Collecting in the Mid-Atlantic States (Johns Hopkins University Press, 1991)

As Illustrator

Illustrated Field Guide to Congenital Heart Disease and Repair (Scientific Software Solutions, Inc, 2004)

Fun With Mammals, by Nancy D. Moncrief with Sonya Wolen (Virginia Museum of Natural History, 1999)

Frommer's Guide to Yellowstone and Grand Teton National Parks (MacMillan Travel, 1998)

Discovering Fossils, by Frank A. Garcia and Donald S. Miller (Stackpole Books, 1998)

The MINTS Book: Model Inquiries into Nature in the Schoolyard, (Virginia Museum of Nat. History, 1997)

Angling Alpine, by J. E. Warren (Alpine County California Chamber of Commerce, 1993)

P. B.'s Quick Index to Bird Nesting, by Philip A. Burns (published by author, 1983)